AF584496

THE LIONS DOWN UNDER

A CELEBRATION OF RUGBY'S FUNNIEST QUOTES AND CARTOONS

Mark Lynch

‘We had started the tour hoping to make about £200 each as the All Blacks (All Golds) had done the previous year. We got nothing and were lucky to get home!’

– Dally Messenger, 1907 Wallaby

• • •

‘A major rugby tour by the British Isles to New Zealand is a cross between a medieval crusade and a prep school outing.’

– John Hopkins

• • •

‘I was busier than an one-armed brick layer in Baghdad.’

– Nick Cummings – Wallaby

OMG!
WAS THAT
TODAY?
LYNCH

‘In my time, I’ve had my knee out, broken my collarbone, had my nose smashed, a rib broken, lost a few teeth, and ricked my back; but as soon as I get a bit of bad luck I’m going to quit the game.’

– J. W. Robinson

• • •

‘Sure there have been injuries and deaths in rugby – but none of them serious.’

– ‘Doc’ Mayhew

• • •

‘Rugby is great. The players don’t wear helmets or padding; they just beat the living daylights out of each other and then go for a beer. I love that.’

– Joe Theismann,
famous American quarterback

WILL HE BE RIGHT FOR SATURDAY, DOC?
LYNCH

‘Rugby is a game for big buggers. If you’re not a big bugger, you get hurt. I wasn’t a big bugger but I was a fast bugger and therefore I avoided the big buggers.’

– Spike Milligan

• • •

‘Ballroom dancing is a contact sport.
Rugby is a collision sport.’

– Heyneke Meyer

• • •

‘I didn’t have to play rugby well,
because I had this voice.’

– Tom Jones

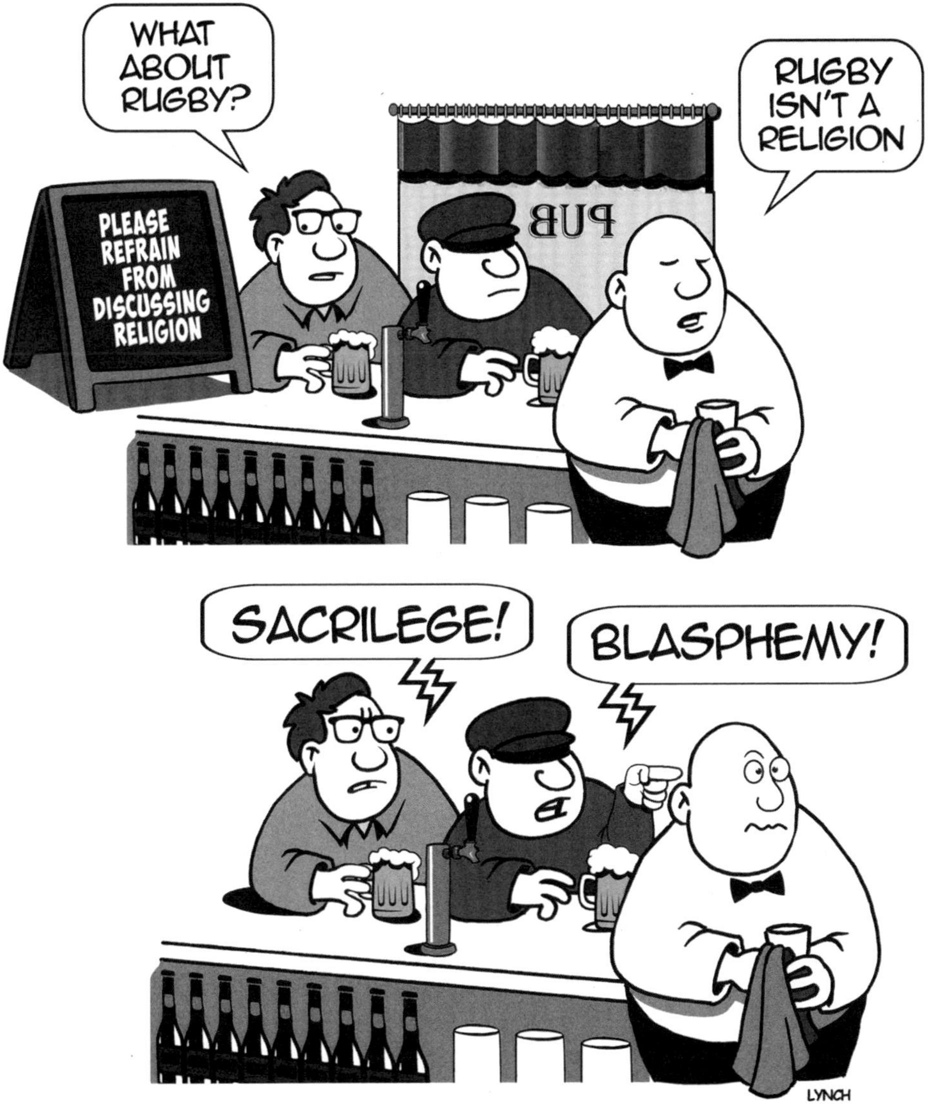

PLEASE REFRAIN FROM DISCUSSING RELIGION
WHAT ABOUT RUGBY?
RUGBY ISN'T A RELIGION

SACRILEGE!
BLASPHEMY!
LYNCH

‘Rugby players are either piano shifters or piano movers. Fortunately, I am one of those who can play a tune.’

– Pierre Danos, French player

• • •

‘You pay the piano player as much as you want but if you don’t pay the piano pusher then the concert doesn’t happen.’

– Dan Crowley, former Australian prop, on player payments

HOW'S MY RUCKING?
LYNCH

‘Rugby players are like lava lamps: good to look at but not very bright.’

– Anonymous

• • •

‘I don’t know why props play rugby.’

– Lionel Weston

• • •

‘Forwards are the gnarled and scarred creatures who have a propensity for running into and bleeding over each other.’

– Peter FitzSimons

SO DO YOU STILL THINK IT WAS A GOOD IDEA TO QUESTION THE LIFESTYLE CHOICES OF THE OPPOSITION PACK DURING A RUCK?

'Bacon and eggs: the chicken is involved,
the pig is committed!'

– Alan Jones, former Wallaby coach,
giving the team some food for thought

• • •

'We had a personality clash. He didn't have one.'

– Peter FitzSimons on Alan Jones

• • •

'C'mon, Stan! Movement is good for weight loss!'

– Alan Jones to Stan Pilecki

'Yep, and you're living proof. No double chin!'

– Pilecki's reply

YNCH

‘A game played by fewer than 15 a side, at least half of whom should be totally unfit.’

– Michael Green

• • •

‘Right! Which ones are the All Blacks?’

– Overheard in a corporate box at Twickenham before an England–New Zealand game

• • •

‘Wife or World Cup? I’m going to miss her.’

– South African supporter’s banner outside Stade de France, 2007

Rugby Types

WHEN I WAS A PROP-FORWARD, I ONCE RAN EIGHTY METRES TO SCORE THE WINNING TRY...CAN YOU SAY THAT?
NOT WITH A STRAIGHT FACE

WE COULD USE A TALL LAD LIKE YOU IN OUR RUGBY TEAM
BUT I KNOW NOTHING ABOUT THE RULES
THAT'S OK...WE NEED REFEREES AS WELL

WARNING!
THE FOLLOWING RUGBY GAME MAY CONTAIN COARSE LANGUAGE, ADULT THEMES, VIOLENCE AND SEXUAL REFERENCES

‘Rugby is a wonderful show: dance, opera and suddenly, the blood of a killing.’

– Richard Burton

• • •

‘I prefer rugby to soccer. I enjoy the violence in rugby, except when they start biting each other’s ears off.’

– Elizabeth Taylor

LYNCH

‘I never comment on referees and I’m not going to break the habit of a lifetime for that prat.’

– Ewan McKenzie

• • •

‘I think you enjoy the game more if you don’t know the rules. Anyway, you’re on the same wavelength as the referee.’

– Jonathan Davies

• • •

‘I’m straighter than that one’

– Referee Nigel Owens,
on a crooked lineout throw.
(Owens was the first openly-gay man
to referee in international rugby)

EXCUSE ME, REF...A FEW OF THE LADS WOULD LIKE TO DISCUSS SOME OF YOUR ON-FIELD-DECISIONS
LYNCH

'He trudg'd along unknowing what he sought,
and whistled as he went, for want of thought.'

– 'The Referee', by John Dryden

• • •

Grandmother or tails, sir?'

– Referee to Princess Anne's son,
Peter Phillips, on the pre-match coin toss

‘F*** you!’ – Player to French referee Didier Mené

‘What did you say?’ – Mené

‘I said “F*** you!”’– Player

‘I decide who f***s me. You’re off!’ – Mené

‘Look what those bastards have done to Wales. They’ve taken our coal, our water, our steel. We’ve been exploited, raped, controlled and punished by the English ... and that’s who you’re playing this afternoon.’

– Phil Bennett

• • •

‘I knew he’d never play for Wales ... he’s tone deaf.’

– Vernon Davies, explaining his son’s choice not to play for Wales

I ONCE REFEREED A TEST MATCH IN WALES
I AWARDED A DUBIOUS PENALTY TO ENGLAND AND THEY KICKED IT TO WIN THE GAME
THAT'S AMAZING! WHEN WAS THAT?
ABOUT FIVE MINUTES AGO
LYNCH

‘Players and spectators at all levels can enjoy sport better if they totally accept two simple rules:
Rule 1: The referee is always right.
Rule 2: In the event of the referee being obviously wrong, Rule 1 applies.’

– Peter Corrigan

• • •

‘The problem with referees is that they just don’t care which side wins.’

– Tom Canterbury

TMO
VIDEO
REF
RUGBY
FOR
DUMMIES
LYNCH

'Lions tours used to represent the apogee in the kind of behaviour usually regarded as hooliganism if perpetrated by the lower orders but high-jinks if it involves young gentlemen of quality.'

– Matthew Engel, *The Financial Times*

• • •

'How did the referee determine when a foul had been committed given that all the players were beating the crap out of each other more or less continuously?'

– Toby Young, *The Spectator*

THE FIRST LIONS TOUR

'Could have been any one of 29 of us.'

– Harlequins player, when quizzed by the referee as to who punched Will Carling

• • •

'You have 15 players in a team. Seven hate your guts and the other eight are making up their mind.'

– Jack Rowell

• • •

'It's no good to talk like Tarzan and play like Jane.'

– Keith Andrews

WHO, MOI?!
LYNCH

‘For an 18-month suspension, I feel I probably should have torn it off. Then at least I could say, look, I’ve returned to South Africa with the guy’s ear.’

– Johan le Roux,
on biting Sean Fitzpatrick’s ear

• • •

‘If I lie in hospital and I hear they are putting someone’s head back on that was ripped off by Schalk, then I’d say: “That’s Schalk, he plays aggressive but he’s not malicious.”

– Peter de Villiers, South African coach

OUR RUGBY CLUB IS ALWAYS ON THE LOOK-OUT FOR NEW BLOOD.... LITERALLY!
YNCH

'I can't remember the names of all the clubs that we went to.'

– Chris Masoe of the Hurricanes on whether he'd visited the pyramids on his visit to Egypt

• • •

'Now spread out, lads, and stick together.'

– Noel Murphy, former Ireland captain

• • •

'I've never had major knee surgery on any other part of my body.'

– Jerry Collins

THEIR ROLLING MAUL DIDN'T REALISE THEY'D CROSSED THE TRY LINE, AND WERE LAST SEEN RUMBLING OUT OF THE GROUND HEADING EAST ON THE MOTORWAY
LYNCH

‘What’s that thing on his head?’

– Garrick Morgan asks a team-mate while watching Mikhail Gorbachev on TV

‘It’s a birthmark.’

– Fellow player

‘How long’s he had that?’

– Morgan

• • •

‘Every time a player like Garrick Morgan leaves rugby to go to rugby league, it lifts the IQ of both codes.’

– Martin Johnson

THE CLUB NUTRITIONIST PUT ME ON A KALE DIET
I FIGURED THE 'K' MUST BE SILENT
LYNCH

‘To play rugby league you need three things: a good pass, a good tackle and a good excuse.’

– Anonymous

• • •

‘The main difference between playing league and union is that now I get my hangovers on Monday instead of Sunday.’

– Tom David

• • •

‘Rugby league is a simple game played by simple people. Rugby union is a complex game played by wankers.’

– Laurie Daley, former league player

IT'S A CALF INJURY
BUGGER! IT'S OFF TO THE VET FOR ME
LYNCH

‘Rugby is a game for the mentally deficient ... that is why it was invented by the British. Who else but an Englishman could invent an oval ball?’

– Peter Cook

• • •

‘They think we’re just a bunch of ignorant Paddies from the bog. Let’s not disappoint them.’

– Stewart McKinney,
Irish player, before a match against England

SPORT
PSYCHOLOGIST
THE
RUGBY
WHISPERER
FAT LOAD OF
GOOD THAT WAS!
I COULD HARDLY
HEAR A WORD
SHE SAID!
LYNCH

'The tactical difference between Association Football and Rugby with its varieties seems to be that in the former the ball is the missile, in the latter men are the missiles.'

– Alfred E. Crawley,
The Book of the Ball, 1913

• • •

'O'Callaghan, you're boring!'

– Referee's infringement call

'You're not too entertaining yourself, ref.'

– Phil O'Callaghan,
former Irish prop

I GET HUNDREDS OF 'LIKES' ON MY SOCIALS
IS THAT LIKE HAVING LOTS OF MONEY IN MONOPOLY?
LYNCH

‘Geez, this fitness thing has got complicated. I just run my blokes till they spew and then take ’em down the pub.’

– Graeme ‘Butch’ McDougall

• • •

‘What do you get out of it?
You get a sore hand and a week’s break.’

– Richie McCaw, on why he doesn’t punch opponents

• • •

‘Rugby and sex are the only things you can enjoy without being good at them.’

– Anonymous

How The Backs see the Forwards

LYNCH

'The forwards: eight handsome, burly guys whom you'll gladly give your beer and food to, and you'd want to marry your daughter. They are intelligent, elegant, sensitive and sweet. Truly the ideal men.

The backs: seven guys who will steal your beer, take advantage of your women folk, barnyard animals and all tubular household objects, regularly take blow dryers on road trips, and wear bikini underpants.

– Rugby positions

How the Forwards see the Backs

‘Rugby backs can be identified because they generally have clean jerseys and identifiable partings in their hair ... come the revolution, the backs will be the first to be lined up against the wall and shot for living parasitically off the work of others.’

– Peter FitzSimons

• • • • •

‘Colin Meads is the kind of player you expect to see emerging from a ruck with the remains of a jockstrap between his teeth.’

– Tom O’Reilly

• • • • •

‘Hey, Ref, count the players, I think Meads ate one!’

– Kel Tremain captaining Hawkes Bay against Colin Meads in the 50s.

A BEHIND-THE-SCENES PREVIEW
INTO THE DARK ARTS VIA-
SCRUM CAM!
LYNCH

‘Brian, what are you going to do for a face when Saddam wants his arse back?’

– Peter Clohessy to
opposing prop Brian Moore

• • •

‘The first half will be even.
The second half will be even harder.’

– Terry Holmes

• • •

‘This is a rugby ball, right?’

– Ciaran Fitzgerald, Irish captain,
attempts to simplify a dressing-room talk

‘Oh Jesus! You’re going too fast for us.’

– Voice from the back

MASSAGE PARLOUR
I'M TELLIN' YOU, CHLOE, THEIR AIN'T ANOTHER HOOKER AROUND THAT CAN MATCH YOUR RUCKING TECHNIQUE!
LYNCH

'Get your retaliation in first!'

– Willie John McBride

• • •

'American football is rugby after a visit from a health and safety inspector.'

– Anonymous

• • •

'Beating NSW is like sex: when it's good, it's great and when it's not, you can always get on the piss.'

– Chris Handy

Rugby Types

IT'S A RUGBY INJURY
I WARNED HIM ABOUT WATCHING THE GAME AT THE OPPOSITION'S PUB!

HONEY, I'M BUSY WATCHING THE RUGBY, CAN YOU TOAST ME SOME MUFFINS?
CERTAINLY, HERE'S TO MUFFINS!

THIS GUY LOOKS PROMISING, 'MAD RUGBY PLAYER WITH A NICE ASS'
LYNCH

‘I once dated a famous Australian rugby player who treated me just like a football: he made a pass, played footsie, then dropped me as soon as he scored.’

– Kathy Lette

• • •

‘In America a guy might wake his partner in the middle of the night to make love. A Kiwi would wake her up to watch the All Blacks on TV.’

– Female reporter, London’s *Daily Telegraph*

‘That is blatantly wrong! Any sensible Kiwi would wake his partner and get her to organise the tea and biscuits so she could watch the game with him.’

– Keith Quinn

THOSE TWO ARE GOING AT IT HAMMER AND TONGS
MY MONEY IS ON THE ONE WITH THE HAMMER
LYNCH

‘Everybody thinks we should have moustaches and hairy arses, but in fact you could put us all on the cover of *Vogue*.’

– Helen Kirk, US rugby player

• • •

‘Whoever said giving birth is the worst pain there is has never seen her team lose the World Cup.’

– Bumper sticker

• • •

‘We used to have a drinking game when we played Wales. Every time the commentator said Jones, Davies or Williams, we’d take a shot. Nobody ever remembered the end of a game.’

– James Noonan

YOU'RE CHAUVINISTIC, MISOGYNISTIC AND A LOUSY REFEREE!
COULDN'T THIS WAIT 'TILL WE GET HOME, HON'?
LYNCH

I hate being called sexy, but I'm a rugby player, so I can't help it.

– Women's rugby T shirt

• • •

A rugby girl is like a normal girl, only cooler!

– Meme

• • •

Maul me, ruck me, make me scrum!

– Bumper sticker

SHOULD WE BE WORRIED ABOUT ALEXA LISTENING IN ON OUR GAME PLAN?
NO, THAT'S A MALE VERSION, IT DOESN'T LISTEN TO ANYTHING
COACH
12
LYNCH

"To win, their 15 players have to have diarrhoea and we will have to put snipers around the field shooting at them and then we have to play the best game of our lives."

– Argentine lock, Juan Martín Fernández Lobbe, on playing the All Blacks.

• • •

"Like 15 mongrel dogs outside a butcher shop."

– Chris (Buddha) Handy describes the All Blacks

I THINK HE FANCIES YOU
LYNCH

'We are not calling them the All Blacks this week. They are New Zealand. New Zealand is a poxy little island in the South Pacific.'

– Scott Johnson, then Welsh assistant coach

• • •

'I apologise to all New Zealanders.
In fact, it's *two* poxy islands in the South Pacific.'

– Johnson again

• • •

'I broke many bones in my rugby career, and I'm only glad that none of them were mine.'

– Peter Fitzsimons, as said to orthopaedic surgeon and now World Rugby chairman Brett Robinson

YOU'RE ACCUSED OF PUNCHING, GOUGING, BITING AND STOMPING
I PREFER THE TERM, MULTI-TASKING
CITING COMMITTEE
LYNCH

‘I don’t like this new law, because your first instinct when you see a man on the ground is to go down on him.’

– Murray Mexted

• • •

‘Leonard! Leonard, you fat bastard! You don’t need a physio, you need a f*****g midwife!’

– Will Carling recalls a sledge from the Irish crowd as prop Jason Leonard was receiving treatment

O'MALLEY! THE CORRECT TERM IS 'TEAM HUDDLE' AND MUST NEVER AGAIN BE REFERRED TO AS, 'A GROUP HUG!'
6
11
LYNCH

‘There’s nothing that a tight forward likes more than a loosie right up his backside.’

– Murray Mexted

• • •

‘He deserved it.’

– Brad Johnstone, Italian coach, on why Peter Stringer was headbutted by his prop

• • •

‘Rugby is a mimic war. When we want real war, we turn to the front of the newspaper.’

– Simon Barnes, *The Times*

RECENT DISCOVERIES IN DNA TECHNOLOGY HAVE IDENTIFIED YOU AS THE PHANTOM PUNCHER DURING A GAME IN 1968... I'LL NEED YOU TO ACCOMPANY ME DOWNTOWN
LICE
POLICE
LYNCH

'Cliff, this must have been a very disappointing result for the All Blacks.'

'Well, they've had very bad luck on tour so far. They missed four easy kicks against the Exeter Amateur Operatic Society, and then of course there was that crippling defeat at the hands of the Derry & Toms soft toy department, so I don't think they can really be fancying their chances against the London Pooves on Saturday.'

– *Monty Python's Flying Circus*, Episode 23.
Interviewer: Michael Palin;
Cliff: Graham Chapman

GAME PLAN
SCORE MORE POINTS THAN THE OTHER TEAM
ANY QUESTIONS?
C
LYNCH

‘Bill, there’s a guy just run on the park with your backside on his chest.’

– Steve Smith to Bill Beaumont,
as Erica Roe streaked at Twickenham

• • •

‘He’d certainly be in the starting line-up for the Easter Island first 15.’

– Phil Kearns commenting on the size
of Schalk Burger’s head

• • •

‘Paddy, do you realise you’re depriving a village back home of an idiot?’

– Eric Rush, to referee Paddy O’Brien

WHILST I ENJOY BEING AT THE GAME, I DO MISS THE PAUSE BUTTON SO I CAN GO AND PUT THE KETTLE ON
LYNCH

'I owe a lot to my parents, especially my mother and father.'

– Tana Umaga

• • •

'I had all the brand new gear right down to the boots with clean white laces. When we got there the coach decided I was too young to play. My mum took me home in tears. I was so upset she let me sleep in my gear that night.'

– Todd Blackadder, aged six

AI RESEARCH
IT'S BAFFLING, WE PROGRAM IT WITH EVERY BIT OF SCIENTIFIC DATA AND INTELLIGENCE KNOWN TO MAN...AND ALL IT WANTS TO DO IS PLAY RUGBY
LYNCH

‘My father used to call that not a tactical kicker but a testicle kicker ... basically a real balls-up.’

– Murray Mexted

• • •

‘Don’t hit him in the honeymoons.’

– Andre Watson, referee

• • •

‘Rugby is a game in which a handful of fit men run around one and a half hours watched by millions who could really use the exercise.’

– Anonymous

OI! RUGGER-BUGGER, FANCY TEN MINUTES IN THE SIN BIN?
LYNCH

'The Holy Writ of Gloucester
Rugby Club demands:
first, that the forwards shall win the ball;
second, that the forwards shall keep the ball; and
third, the backs shall buy the beer.'

– Doug Ibbotson

• • •

'The pub is as much a part of rugby as is
the playing field.'

– John Dickenson

George and the Dragon Pub

HOP IT, YOU LOT! WE DON'T SERVE RUGBY TEAMS HERE

PERHAPS IF WE COULD TALK TO GEORGE INSTEAD
3
9
.YNCH

‘I thought I would have a quiet pint ... and about 17 noisy ones.’

– Gareth Chilcott (on playing his last game)

• • •

‘Beer was invented to stop props taking over the world.’

– Anonymous

• • •

‘It would never have happened in my day, and I’m really upset about that because if it had then I wouldn’t have retired.’

– Gareth Thomas, former Lions captain and gay man commentating on English prop, Joe Marler grabbing Welsh lock Alun Wyn Jones in the nether regions

WHENEVER THE RUGBY IS ON, YOU ONLY HEAR THE THINGS YOU WANT TO HEAR
A BEER SOUNDS LOVELY, THANK YOU
LYNCH

'Thou shalt not kiss thy team-mate on the mouth, even when he hath scored, for such is an abomination unto the IRB, especially he that kisseth in tongues, unless it cometh to pass that thou should play with circular ball, for then it is truly expected of thee.'

– Fourth commandment of rugby

TONIGHT'S TRAINING –
POST-TRY CELEBRATIONS
11
LYNCH

'Thou shalt not pass the ball to a brother thy team-mate about to be smashed by thine enemies, unless it be known to all men that he oweth you money, or hath porked someone dear to your heart, in which case all shall be forgiven and then, verily, thou mayest pass to him right slowly and on high.'

– Ninth commandment of rugby

Last
Will and
Testament
15
LYNCH

Bill McLaren, Scotsman, 1923 – 2010,
BBC commentator, *The Voice of Rugby*:

• • •

'A frank exchange of opinions between the gentlemen of the front row.'

– During an on-field punch-up

• • •

'He's like Bambi on speed.'

– On Simon Geoghegan

• • •

'They say down at Stradey that if you ever catch him, you get to make a wish.'

– On Phil Bennett

CAN I GET A SELFIE WITH YOU, PLEASE?
HERE'S MY AGENTS DETAILS, WE'LL SEE IF WE CAN WORK SOME-THING OUT
LYNCH

• • •

'I'm no hod carrier but I would be laying bricks he was running at me.'

– On Jonah Lomu

• • •

'Born when meat was cheap.'

– On big Vleis Visagie

• • •

'Oh mercy me! What a tackle!
That could've put him in Ward 4!'

– Bill McLaren

'I hope not, Bill, that's a maternity ward.'

– Fellow commentator

CONGRATULATIONS, LAD, YOU'VE BEEN SELECTED TO PLAY FOR THE BARBARIANS
LYNCH

• • •

‘Rugby football is a game for gentlemen of all classes, but never for a bad sportsman in any class.’

– Motto of the Barbarians Rugby Football Club

• • •

‘Rugby is a game for barbarians played by gentlemen. Football is a game for gentlemen played by barbarians.’

– Oscar Wilde

BUT REF, HE CALLED MY MUM A HOOKER! KNOWING FULL WELL SHE WAS A TIGHT-HEAD PROP
4
LYNCH

‘I’ve had four calls from my aunty in the middle of the night calling me a poofter.’

– Frank Bunce appeals to coach John Hart to drop his ‘don’t retaliate’ stance after copping a barrage of punches without responding

• • •

‘They [the All Blacks] kicked the hell out of me in the test. But they were nice blokes.’

– Harold Tolhurst, 1931 Wallaby

‘The Australians were a great crowd. They’d kick your head off on the ground but they were the best chaps in the world off it.’

– Alf Watennan, 1929 All Black

Rugby Types

HELLUVA MAORI-SIDESTEP, BRO!

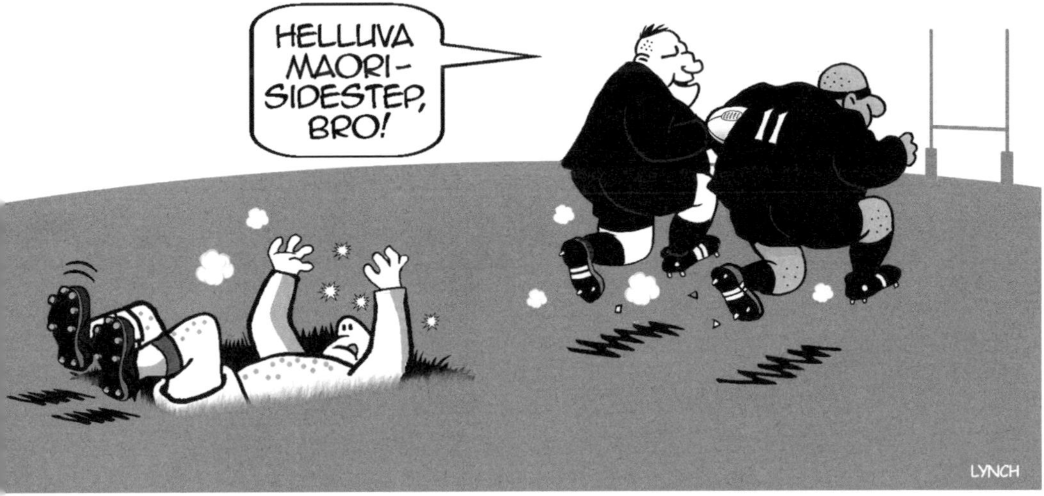

LYNCH

• • •

'I met Jonah Lomu. I never knew how huge he was. I felt like a peasant in a Godzilla movie. "Quickly! Tell the other villagers! We go now."'

– Robin Williams

• • •

'Fijian fullback Waisale Serevi thinks "tackle" is something you take fishing with you.'

– Jonathan Davies

I TOLD HER I'D PREFER TO STAY AT HOME AND WATCH THE RUGBY RATHER THAN GO OUT FOR OUR ANNIVERSARY...SHE SEEMED TO TAKE IT PRETTY WELL
LYNCH

‘Remember that rugby is a team game; all fourteen of you make sure that you pass the ball to Jonah.’

– Anonymous fax sent to the New Zealand team at the 1995 World Cup in South Africa

• • •

‘Me? As England’s answer to Jonah Lomu? Joanna Lumley, more likely.’

– Damian Hopley, 1995

SUPPORTERS TOUR
PUB
PUB
PUB
PUB
PUB
PUB

'I can tell you it's a magnificent sensation when the gap opens up like that and you just burst right through.'

– Murray Mexted

• • •

'Of course it worries me if the All Blacks are invincible. I mean, it stands to reason, if we can't see them, how can we beat them?'

– Unknown English rugby player

BLOODY GOOD PLAYER! BUT TALK ABOUT INJURY PRONE
LYNCH

‘Scorpio: there will soon come a time when your happiness depends on where and whether an enormous man catches a ball.’

– Horoscope from *The Onion*

• • •

‘The only thing you’re ever likely to catch on the end of an English backline is chilblains.’

– David Campese

THOSE TWO OLD DRUNKEN RUGBY-TRAGICS COULD BE US IN TWENTY YEARS
THAT'S A MIRROR!
LYNCH

‘Whoso would be a man, must be non-conformist and preferably play in the pack.’

– Ralph Waldo Emerson

• • •

‘Ja, anyone know where I can get an engine for a Toyota Corolla?’

– Frans Erasmus, late Springbok prop,
on being asked if he had anything to add to
an inspiring team talk

IT WAS A PRETTY NASTY CONCUSSION, WE'LL NEED TO KEEP HIM OVERNIGHT...WILL YOU REQUIRE A LOANER?
LYNCH

You've got to get your first tackle in early, even if it's late.'

– Ray Gravell

• • •

'Right, lads, I want 80 per cent commitment for 100 minutes.'

– Noel Murphy

• • •

'Most footballers are temperamental.
That's ninety per cent temper
and ten per cent mental.'

– Doug Plank

WELL SOMEONE'S GOTTA TALK TO THE FRONT ROW ABOUT THEIR CURRY-NIGHT BONDING SESSIONS

‘I think he’s broken his nose.’

– First commentator, as Sean Fitzpatrick is being led from the field

‘No, I think someone has broken it for him.’

– Second commentator (Fergus Slattery)

• • •

‘Will there be many of them?’

– Willie John McBride, on being told by an Afrikaans publican that he was calling the police

SEEING AS WE'VE GONE CASHLESS, I'LL NEED YOU TO PLAY SCISSORS-PAPER-ROCK, TO SEE WHO KICKS OFF
LYNCH

‘No leadership, no ideas. Not even enough imagination to thump someone in the line-out when the ref wasn’t looking.’

– J. P. R. Williams on a Welsh loss

• • •

‘How’s Stirling Mortlock’s nuts?’

– Female reporter questions Eddie Jones on Mortlock’s groin injury

• • •

‘The winners eat the losers.’

– A Fijian player answers an English reporter’s question, ‘How do you celebrate a victory?’

PERFORMANCE ENHANCING DRUGS ARE A BLIGHT ON THE GAME OF RUGBY

I SAY THAT IF A CHAP CAN'T PERFORM OFF HIS OWN BAT...

...HE SHOULD GIVE THE GAME AWAY

VIAGRA?
TA!
LYNCH

'Do that again, son, and you will live up to your name.'

– Gareth Chilcott to Dai Young

• • •

'Rugby is played by men with odd-shaped balls.'

– Bumper sticker

• • •

'He scored that try after 22 seconds – totally against the run of play.'

– Murray Mexted

GOLDEN
OLDIES
TOURNAMENT
YOU KNOW WHAT THEY SAY ABOUT OLD RUGBY PLAYERS
NOPE!
DANG! I CAN'T REMEMBER EITHER!
LYNCH

‘The job of the Welsh coach is like a minor part in a Quentin Tarantino film: you stagger on, you hallucinate, nobody understands a word you say, you throw up, you get shot.’

– Mark Reason

• • •

‘Nobody ever beats Wales at rugby. They just score more points.’

– Graham Mourie

HE REQUESTED HIS REMAINS BE SPREAD OVER HIS FAVOURITE RUGBY GROUND
HE NEVER SAID ANYTHING ABOUT BEING CREMATED FIRST
LYNCH

'Rugby is a good occasion for keeping thirty bullies far from the centre of the city.'

– Oscar Wilde

• • •

'Those who can play games, they play.
Those who can't play, coach.
Those who can't coach, write.
And those who can't write, commentate!'

– Jim Neilly, BBC commentator

HIS THROWING ARM ISN'T WHAT IT USED TO BE

'The number of people who say,
"Why don't you smile when the camera is on you?"
At least you're not scratching your balls.'

– All Blacks coach Graham Henry

••••

'You guys pair up in groups of three, then line up in a circle.'

– Colin Cooper, Hurricanes coach

CROUCH, BIND, SET!
MOTHER TOLD ME NOT TO MARRY A RUGBY REFEREE

'Look, these *Phantom* comic-swappers and Mintie eaters, these blond-haired flyweights are one thing and we will need them after the hard work's done. But the real stuff's got to be done right here by you blokes.'

– Ross Turnbull, addressing the Wallabies' forwards on the merits of their backs

• • •

'Forwards win games, backs decide by how much.'

– *Planet Rugby*

WHAT A COINCIDENCE, I'VE JUST FINISHED READING YOUR SCATHING ONLINE-REVIEW OF MY REFEREEING IN LAST WEEK'S RUGBY GAME
LYNCH

Murray Deaker: 'Have you ever thought of writing your autobiography?'

Tana Umaga: 'On what?'

• • •

'Fa'- nickname of Scott Quinnell.

• • •

'Everyone knows that I've been pumping Martin Leslie for a couple of seasons now.'

– Murray Mexted

WHAT'S YOUR OPINION OF MY CURRENT FORM?
IT'S USE-LESS!
I KNOW, BUT I'D LIKE TO HEAR IT ANYWAY
LYNCH

'The relationship between the Welsh and the English is based on trust and understanding. They don't trust us and we don't understand them.'

– Dudley Wood

• • •

'Mothers keep their photo on the mantelpiece to stop the kids going too near the fire.'

– Jim Neilly, on the Munster pack

BRIAN HAS TO SHED A FEW KILOS BEFORE THE PRE-SEASON, SO HE'S ON ONE OF THOSE FANCY MEDITERRANEAN DIETS
PIZZERIA
PIZZA
LYNCH

‘Nobody in rugby should be called a genius. A genius is someone like Norman Einstein.’

– Jono Gibbes

• • •

‘What is it with you? Is it ignorance or apathy? He said, “I don’t know and I don’t care.”’

– David Nucifora talking about Troy Flavell

• • •

‘I want to reach for 150 or 200 points this season, whichever comes first.’

– David Holwell

CLUB MASSEUSE
A HAPPY ENDING!? DO I LOOK LIKE WALT DISNEY?
LYNCH

'He's not the sharpest knife in the draw, our Jeremy. He still gets confused why his sister has two brothers but he's only got one.'

– Andy Nicol on Jeremy Guscott

• • •

'A splendid type and a good rugby player ... he is virtually bone from the neck up and needs things explained in words of one letter.'

– British Dominion Office, 1964, describing East African forward Idi Amin

Rugby Types

KEEP PUSHING, HON', AND I'LL POP BACK IN AT HALF TIME
MATERNITY WARD
WE BRING OUT THE KID IN YOU

RUGBY HAS A LOT OF UN-WRITTEN LAWS
AND WHERE ARE THEY KEPT?

BLOODY NIGHT GAMES!

YOU HAVEN'T HEARD THE BEST BIT... NO REF'S OR TMO'S
4
LYNCH

• • •

'Rugby football: Each side is allowed to put in a certain amount of assault and battery and do things to its fellow man which, if done elsewhere, would result in 14 days without the option, coupled with some strong remarks from the Bench.'

– P. G. Wodehouse, *Very Good, Jeeves*,1930

• • •

'A bomb under the West car park at Twickenham on an international day would end fascism in England for a generation.'

– Philip Toynbee, British writer and communist

'Rugby is nonsense, but a serious nonsense.'

– Cliff Morgan

‘Far be it for me to criticise the referee, but I saw him after the match and he was heading straight for the opticians. Guess who he bumped into on the way? Everyone!’

– Ian McLauchlan

• • •

‘Soccer is about spending 90 minutes pretending that you’re injured. Rugby is about spending 80 minutes pretending that you’re not.’

– Anonymous

• • •

Rugby

A great way to meet people since 1823

First published in 2025 by New Holland Publishers

newhollandpublishers.com

A record of this book is held at the National Library of Australia.

ISBN 9781760798376

Managing Director: Fiona Schultz
General Manager/Publisher: Olga Dementiev
Designer: Andrew Davies
Production Director: Arlene Gippert
Printed in China

Keep up with New Holland Publishers:

NewHollandPublishers
@newhollandpublishers